Sam, Fab and Bec

By Debbie Croft

Sam is at the pit.

Sam has a bib.

Sam ran at the pit.

bib

pit

Fab has a bat and a cap.

Fab hits!

Bam! Bam!

cap

bat

Bec is at the mat.

Bec can tip and tap.

Tip, tap, tip, tap!

mat

Sam is fit.

Fab can hit.

Bec tips and taps!

ran

hit

tap

CHECKING FOR MEANING

1. Who has a bib? *(Literal)*

2. What does Fab use to hit the ball? *(Literal)*

3. Why is it important to stay fit? *(Inferential)*

EXTENDING VOCABULARY

cap	Look at the word *cap*. What is another word that has a similar meaning to *cap*?
mat	Look at the word *mat*. What other words do you know that rhyme with *mat*?
tap	Look at the word *tap*. What does *tap* mean in this text? What is another meaning of this word?

MOVING BEYOND THE TEXT

1. Why is the pit filled with sand?

2. In which other sports do you use a bat?

3. Other than sport, what can you do to stay healthy?

SPEED SOUNDS

Cc	Bb	Rr	Ee	Ff	Hh	Nn

Mm	Ss	Aa	Pp	Ii	Tt

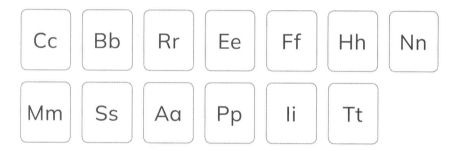

PRACTICE WORDS

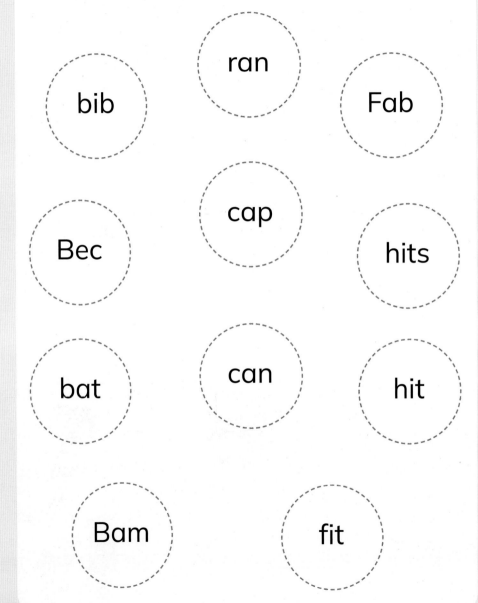

bib

ran

Fab

Bec

cap

hits

bat

can

hit

Bam

fit